**MSP**® **nt**

CW00644719

Managing Successful Programmes Pocketbook

This book was supplied by:

**Wessex House, St. Leonards Road,
Bournemouth, BH8 8QS**
www.cupe.co.uk   **E-mail:** enquiries@cupe.co.uk
Tel:+44 (0)1202 555711

London: TSO

information & publishing solutions

Published by TSO (The Stationery Office) and available from:

Online
www.tsoshop.co.uk

Mail, Telephone, Fax & E-mail
TSO
PO Box 29, Norwich, NR3 1GN
Telephone orders/General enquiries:
0870 600 5522
Fax orders: 0870 600 5533
E-mail: customer.services@tso.co.uk
Textphone 0870 240 3701

TSO@Blackwell and other Accredited Agents

First edition Crown Copyright 2007
Second edition Crown Copyright 2012

First published 2012

ISBN 9780113313532 Single copy ISBN
ISBN 9780113313549 (Sold in a pack of 10 copies)

Printed in the United Kingdom for The Stationery Office

Material is FSC certified. Sourced from fully sustainable forests.
P002473215   c40   02/12

Contents

Acknowledgements

Best Management Practice and the Cabinet Office acknowledge, with thanks, the contribution of Rod Sowden (Aspire Europe Ltd) in the construction of this pocketbook.

In addition, Best Management Practice and the Cabinet Office would like to recognize the contribution of the following individuals who acted as reviewers:

Mike Acaster	Cabinet Office
Grant Avery	KPMG New Zealand
Robert Cole	Centre for Change Management
Geof Leigh	Goaldart Ltd
Ian Santry	Home Office

1 Introduction

Today's organizations exist in a climate where change is ubiquitous. The many, dynamic and contradictory drivers for change include innovations in technology, working practices (including outsourcing and partnerships), mergers, increased demands from regulation and, for the public sector, delivery of policy driven by changing political parties and/or ministers. Whatever the organization, wherever it is located and however it is structured, the rate of change is increasing.

Managing Successful Programmes (MSP®) represents proven good practice in programme management in successfully delivering transformational change, drawn from the experiences of both public and private sector organizations.

1.1 WHAT IS PROGRAMME MANAGEMENT?

MSP defines programme management as the action of carrying out the coordinated organization, direction and implementation of a dossier of projects and transformational activities (i.e. the programme) to achieve outcomes and realize benefits of strategic importance to the business.

Programme management aligns three critical organizational elements:

- Corporate strategy
- Delivery mechanisms for change
- Business-as-usual environment.

It manages the natural tension that exists between these elements to deliver transformational change that meets the needs of the organization and its stakeholders.

1.2   TYPES OF PROGRAMMES

There are three distinct types of programmes:

- ■ Vision-led programme:
  - – Has come into existence to deliver a clearly defined vision that has been created and is sponsored by the top of the organization
  - – Tends to be top down in approach, with cross-functional implications for the organization's operations
  - – Entrepreneurial programmes developing new products and services, that focus on innovation or strategic opportunity offered by the business environment
  - – In the public sector, this could be the translation of political priorities into a programme which will refine and deliver the desired changes
- ■ Emergent programme:
  - – Evolves from concurrent, individual projects that have grown within an organization. There is now recognition that coordination of the projects is necessary to deliver the changes and the desired benefits
  - – Is transitory, as it becomes a planned programme when its vision, context and direction have been defined and established
- ■ Compliance programme:
  - – May also be referred to as a 'must do' programme
  - – The organization has no choice but to change as a result of an external event, such as legislative change
  - – Benefits may be expressed in terms of compliance, achievement and avoidance of negative implications rather than measurable improvements in performance.

In reality, most programmes have a mix of these characteristics, but it is helpful to understand the dominant characteristics of a programme as it will help to develop and optimize the priorities and approach. For example, the benefits for a compliance programme may focus on the avoidance of penalties.

1.3   WHEN TO USE MSP

MSP is highly suitable for business transformation and political/societal change, being an approach designed to accommodate high levels of complexity, ambiguity and risk. Adopting a programme approach is not necessary where something new is delivered within the existing business model. Incremental improvements to an existing product or service would not normally warrant a programme approach, nor is a programme relevant in organizing all the projects within an enterprise solely for prioritizing and allocating resources. Organizations have successfully used MSP, or elements of it, in such situations; however, the programme management framework of MSP is primarily designed to cater for leading and managing transformational change.

For each type of programme, the impact may vary according to whether it is:

■   **Specification-led** Where the change being delivered is based on the making and delivering of new facilities, the programme will tend to be led by the specification of the outputs required – for example, a major capital construction programme. There will be relatively low levels of ambiguity about what the programme is to deliver but there may be high levels of complexity and risk in the delivery. The scope will be reasonably well defined and adjusted according to circumstances. MSP's approach can be used in this type of programme but may need to be scaled down, as some of its elements may not be required.

- **Business transformation** Where the change is more focused on transforming the way the business functions (for example, implementing a new service partnership or moving into a new market), the programme will tend to be vision-led with desired outcomes and associated benefits. There is likely to be ambiguity about the overall implication of the changes; for instance, it may not be known how some parts of the organization will react. The greater the impact on customers and the markets, the greater are the levels of ambiguity and risk. MSP is designed to provide structure for such programmes.

- **Political and societal** Where the change is focused on improvements in society, the level of predictability will be reduced, as there will be many uncontrollable external factors also at play. For example, a change that aims to improve the early education of pre-school-age children in order to increase their likelihood of making a more meaningful contribution to society when they leave full-time education will not only take time to design and introduce but the implications for the students and the economy will not necessarily be controllable or predictable in the long term. The scope may need to be adjusted as ambiguities are clarified and the changes are delivered in steps (tranches) over a number of years. MSP is highly suitable for programmes with a high level of complexity, ambiguity and risk. The programme management framework of MSP is primarily designed to cater for leading and managing transformational change.

Figure 1.1 Programme impact matrix

		Predictability of outcome		
		High	Medium	Low
Focus of the change	Specification-led	Major engineering programmes, e.g. Olympic park Complex products based on known design Large-scale technology replacements	Globalization of technology services Adoption of technology that is new to the organization, e.g. ERP Multi-organization delivery	Pioneering engineering techniques Unproven technology implementation Specification-led organizational change
	Business transformation	Implementation of approaches used in similar organizations, e.g. ISO adoption Process change affecting technology and structures	New products or services to existing market place Changing historical working practices, values and structures Supply chain changes, e.g. outsourcing of services	Diversification of new products into new markets Internal external and customer behaviour Radical restructuring of supply chains
	Political and societal change	Change to current legislation or policies Increases or decreases to investment programmes Predictable or clear stakeholder base	New legislation reacting to societal trends Legislative change to affect socio-economic behaviour Changes to public service delivery models, e.g. health provision	Changes to societal values and behaviour, e.g. criminality Incentive-driven change to lifestyles and economic behaviour Long-term societal effects, e.g. health

© Crown copyright 2007 Reproduced under licence from OGC

Figure 1.1 shows how different types of programme have different impacts on the environment.

Some programmes will be highly complex in nature, but have a reasonably well-defined expectation, i.e. there will be high levels of predictability in terms of outcome even though the journey may be costly and complex. On the other hand, change to societal behaviours over a long period, driven by policy and legislation, will have low levels of predictability due to the long timescales, and the cause and effects may not be fully anticipated as other societal trends develop. The programme impact matrix can be used to decide whether an MSP approach is required or, if not, which programme management techniques could be useful in those circumstances.

1.4 THE MSP FRAMEWORK

Figure 1.2 illustrates the three core concepts of MSP. The outer ring represents the principles, the inner ring reflects the governance themes, and the centre illustrates the transformational flow.

Figure 1.2 MSP framework and concepts

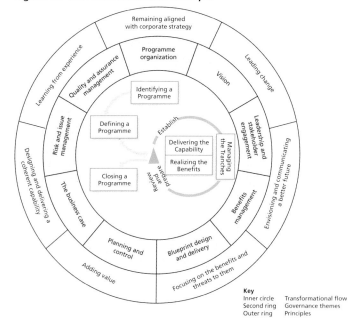

Key

Inner circle	Transformational flow
Second ring	Governance themes
Outer ring	Principles

1.5   THE PRINCIPLES

The principles (outer ring of Figure 1.2) are self-validating, universal and empowering. They apply to all aspects of the delivery of the programme and are as follows:

- **Remaining aligned with corporate strategy** A programme is typically a large investment that should make a significant contribution towards achieving corporate performance targets. A well-managed programme maintains good links with a sometimes-volatile corporate strategy.
- **Leading change** Seeing through change in a programme is a leadership challenge. In addition to the need to manage a large number of complex tasks, people need to be led. It is impossible to move to a better future without clear leadership.
- **Envisioning and communicating a better future** A programme is relevant where there is a need to achieve transformational change, where there is some marked step change or break with the present required in the future capability. In order to achieve such a beneficial future state, the leaders of a programme must first describe a clear vision of that future.
- **Focusing on the benefits and threats to them** Best-practice programme management aligns everything towards satisfying strategic objectives by realizing the end benefits. Thus the programme's boundary, including the projects and activities that become part of the programme, is determined to enable the realization of these end benefits.

  The ultimate success of a programme is judged by its ability to realize these benefits and the continuing relevance of these benefits to the strategic context. If the benefits are of strategic value, then effective risk management is crucial.
- **Adding value** A programme only remains valid if it adds value to the sum of its constituent projects and major activities. If it is found to add nothing, then it is better to close the programme and allow the projects to proceed independently.

- **Designing and delivering a coherent capability** The capability that the programme will deliver is defined in the blueprint. The programme will deliver a coherent organizational capability that is released into operational use according to a schedule that delivers maximum incremental improvements with minimal adverse operational impact.
- **Learning from experience** A programme is a learning organization in that it reflects upon and improves its performance during its life. Good governance requires approaches to managing the different themes that are regularly adjusted and adapted on the basis of experience and results to date. For example, good benefits management encourages stakeholders to identify new opportunities to realize benefits as their awareness and experience increases.

1.6   THE GOVERNANCE THEMES

The themes (Table 1.1) are continuous and apply throughout the programme and are intended to:

- Support the transformational flow and be active in all processes
- Provide a reference point and offer guidance
- Provide tools, techniques and activities
- Recommend areas of focus for each role.

Table 1.1 The governance themes

Governance theme	Summary
Programme organization	Describes the structures for a programme, including the responsibilities and competencies of individuals within those structures.
Vision	Describes the role of the vision statement, its development and contents, and contextual importance to the programme.
Leadership and stakeholder engagement	Describes the need and nature of leadership against the backdrop of stakeholder engagement. Provides tools and techniques to analyse individual and groups of stakeholders with a cycle of activities to maintain engagement and support the communications plans.
Benefits management	Explains how benefits are central to any programme and describes the tools and techniques that can be deployed to ensure the benefits are realized.
Blueprint design and delivery	Describes the criticality of designing the operating model that the programme will deliver. It outlines the concepts of the 'as-is' state, the 'to-be' state, and the step changes required to achieve the target operating model.

Table continues

Table 1.1 *continued*

Governance theme	Summary
Planning and control	Describes the elements that need to be considered to plan, design and deliver the complex set of management activities required to maintain control of the programme, enable project delivery and focus on transition to maintain business as usual during change.
The business case	Describes how the business case will provide the key decision-making information within any programme. It represents the balance between the investment costs and the realizable benefits to be achieved; this helps define the lifecycle of the business case and management controls to be applied.
Risk and issue management	Describes how risk and issue management should be applied to the programme to ensure a structured and systematic approach to identifying and controlling risks and issues. Risk management is based on the Management of Risk (M_o_R®) best-practice framework.
Quality and assurance management	Describes how quality is applied to the programme, describes the areas and activities that characterize quality in the programme and how assurance should be designed and applied to ensure success.

1.7   THE TRANSFORMATIONAL FLOW

As the programme evolves, the transformational flow provides a route through the lifecycle of the programme, from its conception through to delivering the new capability, transitioning to the desired outcomes, realizing the benefits, and finally closing the programme (see Table 1.2). The transformational flow will:

- Detail the programme journey
- Explain the activities to be undertaken in each process
- Provide guidance on responsibilities
- Offer a process-based approach while remaining flexible, defining inputs and outputs for each process
- Ensure that each activity will have an interaction based on one or more governance themes.

Table 1.2 The transformational flow processes

Process	Summary
Identifying a Programme	Takes an outline idea, undertakes an analysis of stakeholders and carries out market consultation to turn it into a business concept that gains strategic support.
Defining a Programme	Develops the vision and undertakes a detailed analysis of the available options. Designs the programme infrastructure to deliver the capability and realize the benefits, resulting in a compelling business case and strategic commitment.

Table continues

Table 1.2 *continued*

Managing the Tranches	Describes the cyclical activities involved in managing and improving the coordinating interface between projects, business change and strategic direction.
Delivering the Capability	Explains how the alignment of the projects and other activities that deliver the blueprint will be managed and builds the capability to enable the business transformation to achieve the benefits.
Realizing the Benefits	Outlines the preparation, delivery and review activities required to take the capability delivered by projects and to embed it within the business operations to realize the benefits.
Closing a Programme	Structured end to the programme, consolidating and embedding the change, closing down all programme activity and notifying stakeholders of programme closure.

2   Governance themes

Governance is the control framework through which programmes deliver their change objectives and remain within corporate visibility and control. A programme needs clear and open governance if it is to be successful. It will need to negotiate the resource it wants, manage the resources made available to it, and adjust to changing organizational contexts whilst delivering its agreed outcomes and benefits. The focus of this section is the core elements of an effective governance framework.

To be effective, programme governance must:

- Give visibility internally and externally
- Clarify the approach
- Deliver consistency in approach
- Apply appropriate levels of control
- Be reviewed regularly
- Improve as it proceeds
- Be integrated with corporate approaches.

Table 2.1 explains the strategies which support the governance themes and how they are applied to the programme.

Table 2.1 Relationship between programme management strategies and delivery mechanisms

Programme management strategy	What the strategy covers	Delivery mechanism
Resource management	Resource to be consumed by the programme. Finances, people, systems, accommodation, facilities and specialisms will all be covered by this strategy	Resource management plan
Monitoring and control	How the programme will monitor progress in terms of expected and actual delivery of outputs, outcomes and key milestones	Programme plan
Information management	How programme information will be catalogued, filed, stored and retrieved, and how the programme will create and manage information	Information management plan

Programme management strategy	What the strategy covers	Delivery mechanism
Quality and assurance management	How the delivery of quality activities will be incorporated into the management and delivery of the programme	Quality and assurance plan
Risk management	How the programme will establish the context in which risks will be identified and assessed, and responses planned and implemented	Risk register
Issue management	How issues will be managed consistently across the programme and how any resulting changes will be managed	Issue register
Stakeholder engagement	Who the stakeholders are, what their interests and influences are likely to be, and how the programme will engage with them	Stakeholder profiles and programme communications plan

Table continues

Table 2.1 *continued*

Programme management strategy	What the strategy covers	Delivery mechanism
Benefits management	The delivery framework for identifying, prioritizing and achieving benefits	Benefit profiles and benefits realization plan

In addition, programme governance should also define the interfaces with other corporate systems (where they exist), for example:

- Finance and accounting
- Human resource management
- Risk management
- Quality systems
- Operations and performance
- Information technology
- Customer and stakeholder satisfaction
- Sourcing and procurement
- Corporate responsibility
- Health and safety
- Environment management
- Contract management
- Legislative compliance
- Information management.

2.1   PROGRAMME ORGANIZATION

Figure 2.1 shows the core programme layers and how they relate to each other. The following sections describe the generic responsibilities for each layer in the programme, together with the key roles.

Figure 2.1 Layering of programme organization, control and reporting

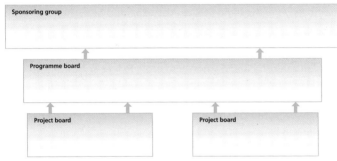

2.1.1   Sponsoring group

The sponsoring group represents those senior managers who are responsible for:

- The investment decision
- Defining the direction of the business
- Ensuring the ongoing overall alignment of the programme to the strategic direction of the organization.

The sponsoring group will appoint the senior responsible owner (SRO) who, as part of the sponsoring group, is likely to be a peer of the other members. The role of the sponsoring group may well be performed by an existing executive committee, or other board of the organization.

2.1.2   Senior responsible owner

The SRO is accountable for the programme, ensuring that it meets its objectives and realizes the expected benefits. The individual who fulfils this role should be able to lead the programme board with energy and drive, and must be empowered to direct the programme and take decisions. They must have enough seniority and authority to provide leadership to the programme team and take on accountability for delivery.

2.1.3   Programme board

Established by the SRO (and often coming into existence following approval of the programme mandate, or possibly the programme brief), the prime purpose of the programme board will be drive the programme forward and deliver the outcomes and benefits. Members will provide resource and specific commitment to support the SRO, who is accountable for the successful delivery of the programme.

The programme board reports to the SRO (see Figure 2.2). Whilst the SRO may delegate responsibilities and action to members of the programme board, its existence does not dilute the SRO's accountabilities and decision-making authority.

Programme board members must take the lead in supporting the authority and control of the SRO over the programme as a whole, including ensuring the appropriate coordination across the projects and activities that comprise the programme.

Figure 2.2 Senior responsible owner and the programme board

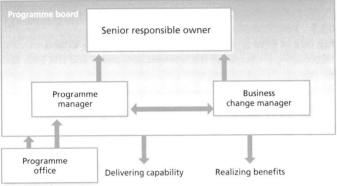

2.1.4 Programme manager

The programme manager is responsible for leading and managing the setting-up of the programme through to delivery of the new capabilities, realization of benefits and programme closure. The programme manager has primary responsibility for successful delivery of the new capabilities and establishing governance. The business change manager (BCM) is responsible for benefits realization via the organizational adoption and usage of the capability and transition to the desired outcome.

The programme manager will normally be appointed as part of forming the team for Defining a Programme, though it is important that someone assumes the role of programme manager when the programme brief and plans for programme definition (programme preparation plan) are being developed in Identifying a Programme.

2.1.5   Business change manager

The role of BCM is primarily benefits-focused. The BCM is responsible, on behalf of the business operations and the SRO, for:

- Defining the benefits
- Defining the future operating state of the business area they represent
- Assessing progress towards Realizing the Benefits
- Achieving measured improvements
- Monitoring performance.

This need to define and realize benefits in terms of measured improvements in business performance means that the BCM must be 'business-side', in order to provide a bridge between the programme and business operations.

The programme manager is responsible for delivering the capability, while the BCM is responsible for realizing the resultant benefits by embedding that capability into business operations, and facilitating business changes to exploit that capability. The individuals appointed to each role must be able to work in close partnership to ensure that the right capabilities are delivered and that they are put to best use.

If a programme is implementing change across different parts of an organization, each should nominate a BCM. An integral part of the BCM role is an intimate knowledge of, and credibility in, the operational business.

2.1.6   Business change team

A business change team can be formed to help each of the BCMs take the stakeholders in their operational areas through the change cycle. Such a team considers the interests of those parts of the organization to be changed and will ensure that those parts are thoroughly prepared for the transition. The team's focus is on helping the operational unit through transition as smoothly as possible. It is a support function for when operational people need the most help.

2.1.7   Programme office

Programmes are major undertakings, often affecting large numbers of people and organizations and generating a substantial volume of information. The nerve centre and information hub of a programme is the programme office. All information, communication, monitoring and control activities for the programme are coordinated through the programme office.

2.1.8   Programme assurance

Assurance is the assessment of specific aspects to generate confidence that the programme is being managed effectively and that it is on track to realize the expected benefits and achieve the desired outcomes. Assurance, like audit, should be carried out independently of the programme management team; this may be by either an internal team and/or an external review team. Assurance may be focused on any number of aspects; please see *Managing Successful Programmes*, chapter 12 for examples of where assurance may be applied.

2.1.9   Other roles

Other optional roles that may be considered:

- Risk manager
- Programme accountant
- Design authority
- Benefits realization manager
- Procurement expertise.

2.2   VISION

A vision is a picture of a better future. In MSP it is the basis for the outcomes and delivered benefits of the programme. As such it is a vital focus and enabler for the buy-in, motivation and activity alignment of the large community of stakeholders involved in any programme.

The vision statement encapsulates the vision and is used to communicate a high-level impression of the desired future 'to-be' state, in contrast to the blueprint, which is a much more detailed description of both the current organization and the changed organization.

It takes time and the involvement of a number of people to draft a clear, compelling and inclusive vision statement. In transformational flow, work on the vision statement should begin soon after the programme mandate has been agreed and the SRO has been appointed. The SRO would assemble a representative group of interested senior management and affected stakeholders and begin building outline vision statement options based on the information in the programme mandate. Once agreed, the outline vision statement is included in the programme brief.

A good vision statement:

- Is written as a future state. It is not to be confused with an objective, strategy, intention or mission, all of which could begin with the word 'To'. Instead, it is a snapshot of the organization in the future.
- Can be easily understood by a wide variety of stakeholders; it is easy to communicate. This means it does not use jargon understood by only one group. It is clear in the vision statement how this better future is different from the present.
- Is written with the broadest groupings of stakeholders as the target audience.
- Describes a compelling future that engages the heart as well as the head. This does not mean it is emotional, but nor is it dry and factual.
- Sets out the current reality as part of the justification for the change – i.e. why the organization cannot stay where it is.
- Matches the degree of transformation change with the boldness of the vision conveyed. Vision statements should motivate everyone and need to do justice to the challenge of transformational change.
- Avoids target dates unless the vision is truly time-dependent.
- Describes a desirable future, in terms of the interests of key stakeholders. Key benefits are implicit.
- Describes a vision that is verifiable but without too many detailed performance targets. A vision statement that contains an inspirational future that is not verifiable can breed scepticism among stakeholders. It should be clear when the organization has arrived at the future state.

- Is sufficiently flexible to remain relevant over the life of the programme. It does not contain too many constraints.
- Provides sufficient context and direction to enable the development of the blueprint.
- Is short and memorable but relevant. Some of the best vision statements are no more than a paragraph. The vision is communicated repeatedly at all kinds of events, and ideally stakeholders can recall it from memory almost word for word.

2.3   LEADERSHIP AND STAKEHOLDER ENGAGEMENT

MSP defines a stakeholder as any individual, group or organization that can affect, be affected by, or perceive itself to be affected by, a programme. There is an inherent link between leadership and stakeholders, which is manifested in the following ways:

- Leaders use the programme vision statement to influence and persuade stakeholders to commit to the beneficial future.
- Business change managers engage their operational stakeholders, leading them through the uncertainty of transition to the new ways of working.
- A focus on benefits recognizes that a 'benefit' is only such when it is perceived to be advantageous by one or more stakeholders. In a community of different interests and attitudes, the leader must engage stakeholders so that benefits are identified, clearly communicated and understood, owned, and realized, and the threats to realizing those benefits are reduced.
- Some stakeholders will be identified as resources within the delivery of the new capability – some with unique or scarce skills and competencies.

MSP provides advice and guidance on:

■ The nature of stakeholder engagement and the need to evaluate and assess their impact and information needs from the programme

■ Defining leadership where this has impacts on how stakeholders are engaged and understood including considering internal politics, individual emotions and motivations

■ Business change management in the wider context where a programme may be seen as a part of a larger strategic change initiative or part of a corporate portfolio of change

■ Communications in the programme (over and above project communications) in line with an engagement strategy.

Figure 2.3 describes the six steps of stakeholder engagement.

Figure 2.3 Stakeholder engagement cycle

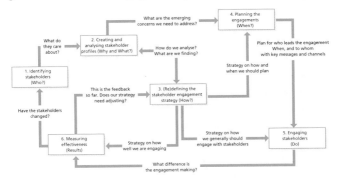

2.3.1   Programme communications plan

The programme communications plan describes what will be communicated, how it will be communicated, when, and by whom, during the programme. It should be designed and implemented as early as possible and then maintained throughout the programme.

Using information from the stakeholder profiles, the activities within the programme communications plan should be designed to:

- Raise awareness amongst all stakeholders of the benefits and impact of the planned outcomes.
- Gain commitment from stakeholders in the target business area(s) to the changes being introduced – thus ensuring the long-term success of the improvements.
- Keep all stakeholders in the target business area(s) informed of progress before, during and after implementation or delivery of programme outcomes.
- Promote key messages from the programme.
- Demonstrate a commitment to meeting the requirements of those sponsoring the programme (the sponsoring group).
- Make communications truly two-way (i.e. a dialogue, not a broadcast) by actively encouraging stakeholders to provide feedback and ensuring that they are informed about the use of their feedback to influence the programme. All types of feedback should be expected, and responses to it carefully considered. Feedback may sometimes be negative, impractical or harshly critical.
- Ensure that all those responsible for projects have an understanding of the scope, nature and outcomes of the programme.
- Promote outcomes to maximize the benefits obtained from the new business operations.

Successful communications are based on four core elements:

- **Stakeholder identification and analysis** Send the right message to the right audience
- **Message clarity and consistency** Ensure relevance and recognition, and engender trust
- **Effective system of message delivery** Get the right messages to the right stakeholders in a timely and effective way
- **Feedback collection system** Assess the effectiveness of the communications process.

2.4   BENEFITS MANAGEMENT

Benefits management is at the very heart of programme management: programmes are primarily driven by the need to deliver benefits. This is achieved by projects creating outputs, which build capabilities, which transition into outcomes that serve the purpose of realizing benefits for the organization. However, it is likely that the programme will have some negative impacts as well as improvements. Where a negative effect of the change can be forecast, then this is termed as a dis-benefit. Benefits and dis-benefits can be defined as follows:

- A **benefit** is the measurable improvement resulting from an outcome perceived as an advantage by one or more stakeholders, which contributes towards one or more organizational objective(s).
- A **dis-benefit** is the measurable decline resulting from an outcome perceived as negative by one or more stakeholders, which detracts from one or more organizational objective(s).

Organizational objectives in this instance may be corporate objectives that are aligned with and delivered by the programme. The differences between outputs, capabilities, outcomes and benefits are summarized in Table 2.2.

Table 2.2 Differences between outputs, capabilities, outcomes and benefits

	Output	Capability	Outcome	Benefit
Description	The deliverable, or output, developed by a project from a planned activity	The completed set of project outputs required to deliver an outcome; exists prior to transition	A new operational state achieved after transition of the capability into live operations	The measurable improvement resulting from an outcome perceived as an advantage by one or more stakeholders and which contributes towards one or more organizational objective(s)

	Output	Capability	Outcome	Benefit
Rationale	Answers at least in part the fundamental question 'What do we need to create to enable the change?'	Answers the question 'What will we need to have in place to enable the new operating state?'	Answers the question 'What is the desired operational state of the organization using these new things?'	Answers the question 'Why is this justified?' (i.e. it explains what a programme delivers)
Example	An individual component of an e-commerce system, application, hardware, new business processes training etc.	An e-commerce system tested and ready to go into operation and with trained staff	Transformed client service organization, faster processing, fulfilling and charging for web-based orders	Increased sales revenues of x%

Programmes normally serve to deliver corporate objectives.
Figure 2.4 illustrates how:

- ▦ The corporate objectives drive the development of the programme vision
- ▦ The vision is expanded into a blueprint for the future organization
- ▦ The blueprint defines what the projects need to create
- ▦ The projects deliver outputs which create capabilities
- ▦ The capabilities are transitioned into outcomes
- ▦ The outcomes enable the realization of benefits
- ▦ The benefits are then achieved and contribute to the achievement of the corporate objectives.

Figure 2.4 Strategic context of benefits management within a programme

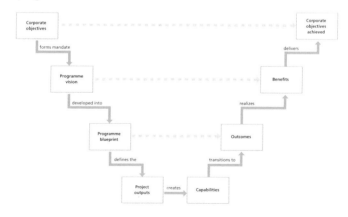

Given its importance to the programme, it is not surprising that benefits management drives many aspects of programme management (see Figure 2.5), including:

- Aligning and validating the integrity of the blueprint against the projects, activities and associated organizational changes needed to deliver the new capabilities and benefits
- Defining the aggregate of achieved benefits, expected benefits, costs to date and expected cost against the business case; providing a crucial test of the ongoing viability of the programme
- Prioritizing benefits to allow the programme to create maximum value under given constraints and make the right trade-off decisions if required
- Planning the programme (benefits realization is a major foundation for this aspect)
- Engaging with stakeholders to understand impact and helping win support
- Defining what is a fit-for-purpose capability, establishing what the critical quality-checking mechanisms throughout the programme would be and checking that they are aligned with the requirements in the blueprint
- Informing end-of-tranche reviews to enable decisions on changes to the programme going forward and underlying governance to be made
- Ensuring that the costs associated with Delivering the Capability are balanced with the value of the benefits in the business case
- Monitoring the risks and issues that may impact benefits realization.

Figure 2.5 Benefits management interfaces

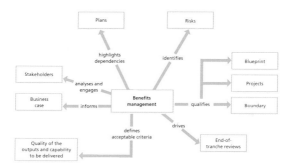

2.4.1   Benefits categorization

Categorizing benefits can help organizations to better model
their priorities and planning and ensure that there is a balanced
portfolio of benefits. By categorizing benefits effectively,
organizations are able to:

- Balance the mix of benefits that are being sought and the
  associated risk profiles
- Enable effective reporting and tracking by category
- Identify potential overlaps of benefit counting
- Understand the impact of changes on different parts of
  the organization
- Track the relationship between objectives and benefits
- Help to manage changes to priorities within the programmes.
  If there is a strategic change in the value types being sought,
  the programme will be more agile in its ability to see the
  impact across the programme

- Help to create a common set of terminology for referring to benefits and bring greater transparency
- Enable a portfolio-level view of benefits across programmes and projects through consistency.

There are many different ways to categorize benefits. The following benefit categories are well established, but they are not exhaustive.

- Value
- Financial impact
- Corporate objective
- Stakeholder impact
- Timeline
- Level of risk.

Figure 2.6 Benefits management cycle

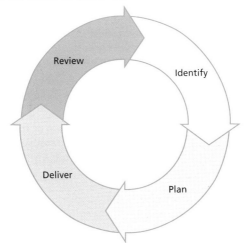

Figure 2.6 shows a generic four-step cycle for managing benefits on any programme.

2.5   BLUEPRINT DESIGN AND DELIVERY

The programme's vision statement provides early and valuable information as a description of the desired outcomes in customer-focused terms. As it is a description at a summary level, it needs to be expanded and developed into a blueprint, which evolves and is refined during the lifecycle of the programme. It is the blueprint that provides a usable basis for modelling benefits and designing the projects dossier.

The blueprint is not concerned with how to get to the future state. The 'how' is dealt with when designing the projects dossier. During Defining a Programme, a number of scenarios will be considered for the final outcome of the programme along with the options for delivering these scenarios. The optimum scenario and delivery option for achieving the final desired outcome is selected. This is reviewed over the programme lifecycle to ensure that the outcome and its solutions remain optimal.

The new capability occurs when the outputs from projects are ready for operational use – once transition is completed and the outcomes have been achieved.

Figure 2.7 shows the nature of the collaboration of the blueprint with other themes. Its delivery is carried out iteratively with benefits management until an acceptable business case starts to emerge.

Figure 2.7 Blueprint design and delivery in collaboration with other themes

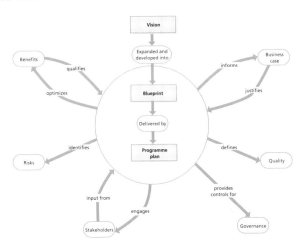

The programme manager is responsible for organizing activities to ensure the blueprint is appropriately authored and signed off. Where the programme manager and BCMs have suitable skills and experience, they can be the authors of the blueprint. Where they don't, it is the responsibility of the programme manager, assisted by the BCMs, to engage appropriately skilled and knowledgeable people as the authors.

The POTI model sets a high-level scope of what must be included and integrated in an effective blueprint:

■ **P** – Processes, business models of operations and functions including operational costs and performance levels

- **O** – Organizational structure, staffing levels, roles, skills requirements, organizational culture, supply chain and style
- **T** – Technology, buildings, IT systems and tools, equipment, machinery and accommodation
- **I** – Information and data required for the future business operations and performance measurement.

Each programme has to plan and manage the journey from where the organization is today to the future as outlined in the vision statement. An understanding of the current state and the gap (the difference between current and future states) is essential to be able to effectively explore alternative approaches to delivering the new capability.

The initial analysis of the gap is a comparison between the current organization (described in the current 'as-is' state section of the blueprint) and the design for the future organization (described in the future 'to-be' state section of the blueprint).

Elements of the blueprint, such as processes, technology etc., are compared as they are now with how they need to be. These are high-level descriptions; more detailed analysis will be carried out by the projects.

In MSP, the programme plan is designed to deliver the new capability in tranches. These step changes in capability should be carefully planned to support the realization of the appropriate, desired benefit(s). A tranche:

- Is made up of one or more projects or activities
- Delivers a step change in capability for the organization, as described in the intermediate blueprint
- Includes transition activities to achieve the outcomes defined for the tranche

■ Provides a control point at which the programme can be re-directed or stopped.

Figure 2.8 shows a sample programme schedule indicating the grouping of projects into tranches and the review points.

Figure 2.8 Example of a programme schedule

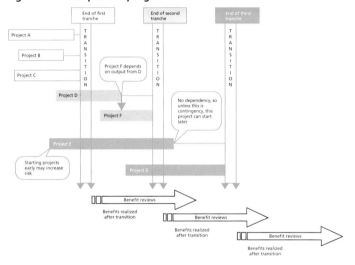

2.6   PLANNING AND CONTROL

Planning and control are key to the success of any transformation programme and should be seen as distinctly separate concepts and activities.

2.6.1   Programme planning

The preparation of the programme plan involves:

- Processing large amounts of information
- Extensive consultation
- Building the plan.

During its early iterations the programme plan will include many unknowns and a high level of ambiguity.

Developing the programme plan should develop and include:

- Resources
- Resource management strategy and plan
- Risk management
- Projects dossier
- Deadlines and constraints
- Scheduling
- Priorities.

Figure 2.9 shows the various contributions made to the programme plan during its development.

Figure 2.9 Contributions to the programme plan

2.6.2   Programme control

Programme control provides supporting activities and processes that run throughout the lifecycle of the programme to:

- Refine and improve delivery
- Minimize the impact of ambiguity
- Bring certainty wherever possible
- Justify the continuance of the programme.

The management and control of the programme should be based on experiences from the previous tranches.

Programme control should consider and develop:

- Monitoring and control strategy
- Dependency management
- Starting projects
- Integration of information
- Progress monitoring
- Project control
- Planning and controlling transition.

2.6.3   Transition management

Whilst an estimate of the length of the transition period should be considered when developing the overall programme plan, more detailed transition planning is not practical until sufficient progress has been made in each individual tranche. Detailed transition planning requires both knowledge of the specific project outputs and the state of readiness of the operations which are due to change.

MSP defines three phases of transition that should be planned for:

- Pre-transition
- Transition
- Post-transition.

For more information on transition management, see section 3.5 on Realizing the Benefits.

2.7 THE BUSINESS CASE

In MSP the business case provides the vital test of the viability of the programme. It answers the question 'Is the investment in this programme still worth it?' The business case evolves from the early documents, e.g. programme mandate and programme brief, and develops throughout the lifecycle, providing a critical decision tool.

Figure 2.10 Validating the business case

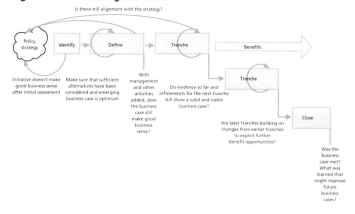

It provides more than the basis for initial approval to start the programme. It is actively maintained throughout the programme, and is continually updated with new information on benefits, costs and risks.

The business case presents the optimum mix of information used to judge whether or not the programme is (and remains) desirable, viable and achievable. Developing and maintaining the business case includes:

- **Genesis of a programme business case** As the suggested business case in the original programme mandate gains detail, it becomes the outline business case in the programme brief, and then on to the full business case that is updated as the programme proceeds.
- **Detailing the contents of the full business case** This involves setting out costs, the planned benefits and the risk profile of the programme, to assess programme viability.
- **Regular reviews of the business case** These are conducted by the programme manager and the business change manager with support from the programme office. The business case should also be formally validated (reviewed and re-accepted) at the end of each tranche by the programme board and senior responsible owner.
- **Managing the business case** It is important to check to what extent the programme can realize the expected benefits, and whether changes to the cost-benefit profile will alter the status and relative priority of the programme in relation to meeting the corporate strategic objectives.

Figure 2.10 shows how the business case is formally validated (reviewed and re-accepted) at the end of each tranche.

2.8   RISK AND ISSUE MANAGEMENT

MSP defines a risk as an uncertain event (or set of events) which, should it occur, will have an effect on the achievement of objectives. This effect need not be detrimental. A risk can be either a threat (i.e. an uncertain event that could have a negative impact on objectives or benefits), or an 'opportunity' (i.e. an uncertain event that could have a favourable impact on objectives or benefits).

Issues are events that have happened, were not planned and required management actions. Risks, should they occur, become issues.

The task of programme risk management is to ensure that the programme makes cost-effective use of a risk management cycle that includes a series of well-defined steps. The aim is to support better decision-making through a good understanding of risks and issues and their likely impact.

Risks and issues can emerge from a variety of sources – for example:

- Benefits management, transition activities, costs, scope and timescales
- Dependencies, constraints, assumptions, quality of operations, resources and programme deliverables
- Anything that cannot be resolved within a project, or issues common to more than one project
- Stakeholders, organization and programme staff, and third parties
- Degradation of operational performance beyond acceptable levels
- Ambiguity or lack of knowledge about the 'as-is' state, interim state and the desired end state
- Other projects and programmes under way within the organization.

Table 2.3 shows four perspectives to risk management, which reflect the following types of risk that a programme will be required to manage.

Table 2.3 Risk management perspectives

Strategic	Changes at the strategic level can affect the programme, its interdependencies with other initiatives and ultimately its outcomes and benefits realization.
Programme	Programmes focus on delivering benefits to the organization and often affect a wide variety of stakeholders both internally and externally, positively and negatively. Risk management for a programme must be designed to work across organizational boundaries in order to accommodate these differing interests and ensure that stakeholders are engaged appropriately.
Project	The project outputs within a programme are the vehicles for delivering the programme outcomes and benefits; therefore, much of the focus of risk and issue management within a programme is from the project perspective. The programme should set the risk and issue management standards for the project and then give staff the authority to manage their risks and issues within these parameters.
	To manage the risks to projects well, the programme needs to ensure that each project brief outlines the risks from the perspective of the programme and then requests that the project provides regular feedback to the programme's risk management activities.

Table continues

Table 2.3 *continued*

Operational	As projects deliver their outputs, the transition to new ways of working and new systems can lead to further sources of risk. For example, during a handover process, risks and issues could arise from the need to maintain operational stability as well as the integrity of the systems, infrastructure and support services. Transition must hence be properly planned, managed and resourced.

2.8.1   Principles of risk management

The key principles for risk management at programme level are that it:

- Aligns with objectives
- Fits the context
- Engages stakeholders
- Provides clear guidance
- Informs decision-making
- Facilitates continual improvement
- Creates a supportive culture
- Achieves measurable value.

2.8.2   Managing risks in a programme

Before the risk management cycle (see Figure 2.11) can operate, the specific arrangements for managing risk need to be specified:

- Risk management strategy
- Risk appetite
- Tolerance thresholds
- Assumptions

- Early-warning indicators
- Risk register content
- Threat and opportunity
- Evaluating risks
- Risk aggregation
- Proximity
- Progress reporting.

Figure 2.11 Programme risk management cycle

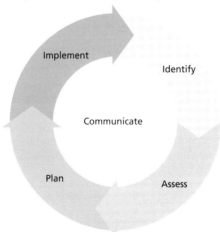

2.8.3 Responses to risks

- Avoid a threat or exploit an opportunity
- Reduce a threat or enhance an opportunity
- Transfer the risk (threat or opportunity)
- Share the risk (threat or opportunity)

- Accept the risk
- Prepare contingent plans.

2.8.4   Managing issues in a programme

Issues can occur at any point from the launch of the programme at the beginning of Identifying a Programme to when the programme closes. Some issues may be unresolved at the end of the programme, and responsibility for these may need to be transferred to operational management.

An issue is a relevant event that has happened, was not planned and requires management action. The action required may be to fix a problem or to change the boundary of the programme. An issue generally emerges from one of a number of sources, for example:

- Constraints identified at the outset of the programme
- Within the programme itself
- In operational areas to be changed by the programme, where these have a consequential impact on the programme
- From an escalation of a programme's constituent projects
- As generated by stakeholders
- Other sources external to the programme (e.g. changes to corporate strategy or conflicts with other concurrent change initiatives).

Issues that occur in a project may need to be escalated if they fall outside the project's tolerance levels set by the programme. Issue management in a programme needs to cover all of these circumstances.

A common cause of overload in a programme is when it tries to manage the project issues directly and does not effectively manage escalation and delegation. However, the programme manager does need to be satisfied that the project teams are managing issues to a satisfactory standard and that the aggregated impact on the programme from all issues in all its projects is understood and acceptable.

Issues can typically be classified into one of the following three types:

- ◼ A previously identified risk that has now materialized and requires appropriate issue management action
- ◼ A request for change to some aspect of the programme, an operation or a project
- ◼ A problem affecting all or part of the programme in some way.

Figure 2.12 Issue management cycle

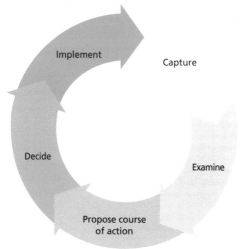

Figure 2.12 shows the issue management cycle which comprises five steps for managing issues.

2.8.5   Change control

Programmes are inherently about delivering change, but they do not work in isolation, and changes are happening to the environment they are delivering to all the time. This can result in changing business requirements, reactions to unplanned events or failures, and loss of stakeholder confidence, all of which can affect the ability of the programme to deliver its objectives. There is a particular risk that small changes across a number of projects may conflict, and because of their apparent insignificance they may pass through unnoticed.

The basic steps of change control are:

- Capture the change and define why it is needed
- Allocate a priority so that the urgency is understood
- Assess the impact across the programme
- Analyse the options and test the potential solutions
- Authorize the resolution that is agreed (which could include no action)
- Implement the change and monitor the effects of the change for deviations from what is anticipated
- Review the effectiveness and update associated documentation.

All changes should undergo an assessment that considers their impact on at least the following:

- Programme plan
- Blueprint
- Benefits
- Projects dossier.

2.8.6   Configuration management

The purpose of configuration management in a programme is to control the development of, and changes to, items that are important to the programme. These items include programme management documentation as well as the assets, products and services created by the programme. Configuration management covers the programme's dependencies on items outside of its control as well as those within the programme.

There are five basic processes involved in programme-level configuration management:

1.   Planning

2.   Identifying

3.   Controlling

4.   Status accounting

5.   Verifying.

2.9   QUALITY AND ASSURANCE MANAGEMENT

The purpose of quality and assurance management is to ensure that all management aspects of the programme are working appropriately and that it stays on target to achieve its objectives. If a programme does not apply quality and assurance effectively to its management activities, then it is less likely to achieve its objectives and deliver the anticipated value and benefits.

Quality and assurance are defined as follows:

■   **Quality** is defined as the totality of features and inherent or assigned characteristics of a product, person, process, service and/or system that bears on its ability to show that it meets expectations or stated needs, requirements or specification.

■ **Assurance** is the systematic set of actions necessary to provide confidence to the SRO and stakeholders that the programme remains under control and on track to deliver and that it is aligned with the organization's strategic objectives.

Quality and assurance management must run continuously throughout the life of a programme; achieving the right level of quality must be an integral part of all the day-to-day activities of the programme.

The programme management principles describe the characteristics of a successful programme and act as critical success factors that apply to all programmes. Therefore, application of and adherence to the principles is essential for the programme to achieve a successful conclusion. To this end, the principles act as the focal point for establishing the critical things that the programme must do to be successful, and quality management makes sure that the programme is doing the right things to assure their achievement.

Whereas the programme principles set out the areas that are critical to the success of a programme, the scope of quality is broader. It covers eight process areas that require management review of their effectiveness in supporting the achievement of the programme objectives.

A number of these processes are covered as part of the MSP governance themes and associated strategies; however, these are areas of particular importance that can cut across a number of themes and strategies, which is why they are being emphasized here in their own right. This is not an exhaustive list, but it provides useful scope for setting out the programme strategy for quality.

The emphasis is on management for all the topics, because good management requires good processes to be in place. The one exception is programme leadership, which is relevant across all the management areas.

Figure 2.13 summarizes the key elements to consider when developing and deploying quality and assurance management in programmes.

Figure 2.13 Scope of programme quality

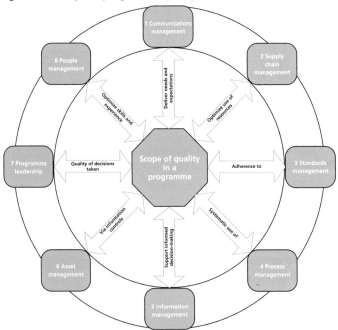

Assurance management principles

There are five assurance management principles:

- ▪ Independence
- ▪ Integration
- ▪ Linkage to major decision points
- ▪ Risk-based activity
- ▪ Action and intervention.

Assurance management techniques

There are a number of techniques that can be used to help assure that the programme is being delivered optimally; that is to say, in the most appropriate and effective way for the achievement of its purpose and objectives:

- ▪ Audit
- ▪ Effectiveness of measurements
- ▪ Assurance reviews
- ▪ Maturity assessments using the Portfolio, Programme and Project Management Maturity Model (P3M3®)
- ▪ Gated reviews.

The P3M3 provides a framework with which organizations can assess their current performance and put in place improvement plans.

A key element of the quality of programme management is information management. The programme will need to have configuration management in place; MSP recommends that this is held in three baselines, as shown in Table 2.4.

Table 2.4 Information baselines

Information baseline	Description of purpose
Boundary	Those which set out the direction and the scope of the programme
Governance	Those that set the standards and frameworks within which the programme will be delivered; defines 'how' the programme will be managed
Management	Those that are created and used to manage the delivery of the programme; defines 'what' activities will be undertaken by 'whom' to deliver the programme.

In addition, there is a need to ensure adequate information security is applied; this should ensure that appropriate controls provide for:

- Compliance
- Integrity
- Availability
- Confidentiality
- Currency.

3 Transformational flow

MSP programmes deliver transformational business change. The transformational flow describes how this is achieved. There are a number of key processes that take the programme from an idea through to delivery (see Figure 3.1).

Figure 3.1 Overview of the transformational flow

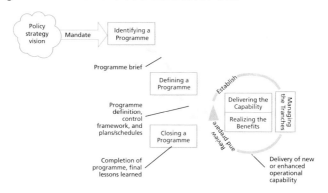

3.1 IDENTIFYING A PROGRAMME

When the programme mandate is signed off, the Identifying a Programme process can begin. The process consists of a number of steps that take an initial or emerging idea or need and frame it into a tangible concept that the business can support through the Defining a Programme process.

3.1.1   Steps

1. Sponsor the programme
2. Confirm the programme mandate
3. Appoint the SRO and programme board
4. Produce the programme brief
5. Develop the programme preparation plan
6. Independent review
7. Approval to proceed.

3.2   DEFINING A PROGRAMME

Defining a Programme takes the concepts that evolve during Identifying a Programme and develops a compelling business proposition that gains the commitment of the sponsoring group and stakeholders. This process provides the basis for deciding whether to proceed with the programme.

The business case and governance for the programme are developed during this process. The governance defines the strategies for quality and assurance, monitoring and control, information management, stakeholders, risks and issues, benefits and resources. The various programme approaches are contained in the strategies, and plans and schedules (covering risk management, communications, benefits realization, resources, quality etc.) are developed to provide information on the resources, dependencies and timescales for delivery of capability and realization of benefits.

A key activity is the development of the blueprint and the investigation of the options available, and the options for delivery.

The inevitable trade-off between resources, costs, quality, timings and benefits requires agreement between the sponsoring group and SRO. At the completion of Defining a Programme, formal approval is required from the sponsoring group and SRO to proceed with the programme.

Figure 3.2 is an example of how the blueprint, benefits maps and projects dossier might be developed during Defining a Programme.

Figure 3.2 Developing the basis of an acceptable business case

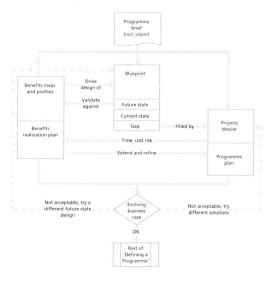

3.2.1 Steps

1. Establish the infrastructure for Defining a Programme
2. Establish the team to define the programme
3. Identify and analyse the stakeholders
4. Refine the vision statement
5. Develop the blueprint
6. Develop the benefit profiles
7. Model the benefits and refine the profiles
8. Validate the benefits
9. Develop the projects dossier
10. Identify tranches
11. Design the programme organization
12. Develop the governance arrangements
13. Develop the programme plan
14. Develop and confirm programme business case
15. Consolidate the programme definition
16. Prepare for first tranche
17. Approval to proceed.

3.3   MANAGING THE TRANCHES

The purpose of the Managing the Tranches process is to implement the defined programme management governance strategies for the programme, ensure that the capability delivery is aligned to the strategic direction of the organization, and enable the release of benefits. This accepts that, as the programme progresses, this will need to be adapted and refined to assure the effective delivery of the tranches and the final outcomes.

A key principle of the Managing the Tranches process is to maintain the balance between the rate of change being offered by the Delivering the Capability process and the rate of change that the operational areas can cope with. This is managed through the Realizing the Benefits stage which aligns the programme with the evolving and changing strategic needs of the organization.

Unlike some of the activities in other processes, which tend to happen in a logical sequence, the activities in Managing the Tranches may recur or happen concurrently. Most of the activities are linked to the governance themes and are intended to trigger the cycles. For example, you do not 'manage risks and issues' once: this is a day-to-day activity that occurs throughout the tranche.

3.3.1   Steps

1. Establish the tranche

2. Direct work

3. Manage risks and issues

4. Control and delivery of communications

5. Undertake audits and assurance reviews

6. Maintain alignment between programme blueprint and business strategy objectives

7. Maintain information and asset integrity

8. Manage people and other resources

9. Procurement and contracts

10. Monitor, report and control

11. Transition and stable operations

12. Prepare for next tranche

13. End-of-tranche review and close.

3.4   DELIVERING THE CAPABILITY

The Delivering the Capability process covers the activities for coordinating and managing project delivery according to the programme plan. Delivery from the projects dossier provides the new outputs that enable the capabilities described in the blueprint. The activities of Delivering the Capability are repeated for each tranche of the programme.

This process delivers the capability defined in the blueprint through the projects defined in the projects dossier. The detail in the blueprint provides the input requirements for the projects, which adopt the strategic requirements and undertake detailed specification and design to deliver the outputs that create the capability needed to achieve the outcomes and deliver the benefits.

3.4.1   Steps

1. Start projects

2. Engage stakeholders

3. Align projects with benefits realization

4. Align projects with programme objectives

5. Governance: manage and control delivery

6. Close projects.

3.5   REALIZING THE BENEFITS

The purpose of the Realizing the Benefits process is to manage the benefits from their initial identification to their successful realization. The activities cover monitoring the progress of the projects to ensure that the outputs are fit for purpose and can be integrated into operations such that the benefits can be realized.

Realizing the Benefits incorporates the planning and management of the transition from old to new ways of working and the achievement of the outcomes, whilst ensuring that the operational stability and performance of the operations are maintained. The activities of this process are repeated as necessary for each tranche of the programme.

Three distinct sets of activities are covered in this process:

- **Manage pre-transition** The analysis, preparation and planning for business transformation
- **Manage transition** Delivering and supporting the changes
- **Manage post-transition** Reviewing progress, measuring performance and adapting to change.

3.5.1   Steps

1. Manage the pre-transition

- Establish benefits measurements
- Monitor benefits realization
- Plan transition
- Communicate the change
- Assess readiness for change

2. Manage transition

- Initiate transition
- Establish support arrangements
- Enact transition
- Review transition
- Manage outcome achievement

3. Manage post-transition

- Measure benefits
- Remove access to legacy working practices and systems
- Respond to changing requirements
- Monitor and report benefits realization.

3.6   CLOSING A PROGRAMME

The purpose of Closing a Programme is to ensure the end goal of formally recognizing the programme is completed. This is when the programme has delivered the required new capabilities described in the blueprint and has assessed the outcomes via benefit measures.

3.6.1   Steps

1. Confirm ongoing support is in place
2. Confirm programme closure
3. Notify programme is about to close
4. Review programme
5. Update and finalize programme information
6. Provide feedback to corporate governance
7. Disband programme organization and supporting functions.

4   MSP information

Table 4.1 provides a list of all of the information documents within MSP and a summary of the purpose of each document.

Table 4.1 Information documents within MSP

Title	Purpose
Benefit profile	Used to define each benefit (and dis-benefit) and provide a detailed understanding of what will be involved and how the benefit will be realized
Benefits management strategy	Defines the approach to realizing the benefits and the framework within which benefits realization will be achieved
Benefits map	Illustrates the sequential relationship between benefits
Benefits realization plan	Used to track realization of benefits across the programme and set review controls
Blueprint	Used to maintain focus on delivering the required transformation and business change
Business case	Used to validate the initiation of the programme and the ongoing viability of the programme

Title	Purpose
Information management plan	Sets out the timetables and arrangements for implementing and managing the information management strategy
Information management strategy	Describes the measures, systems and techniques that will be used to maintain and control programme information
Issue management strategy	Used to describe the mechanisms and procedures for resolving issues
Issue register	Used to capture and actively manage programme issues
Monitoring and control strategy	Defines how the programme will apply internal controls to itself
Organization structure	Description of the management roles, responsibilities and reporting lines in the programme
Programme brief	Used to assess whether the programme is viable and achievable
Programme communications plan	Sets out the timetable and arrangements for implementing and managing the stakeholder engagement strategy
Programme definition document	A document that is used to consolidate or summarize the information that was used to define the programme

Table continues

Table 4.1 *continued*

Title	Purpose
Programme mandate	Used to describe the required outcomes from the programme, based on strategic or policy objectives
Programme plan	Used to control and track the progress and delivery of the programme and resulting outcomes
Programme preparation plan	A plan that details how Defining a Programme will be undertaken
Projects dossier	Provides a list of projects required to deliver the blueprint, with high-level information and estimates
Quality and assurance plan	Sets out the timetable and arrangements for carrying out the quality and assurance strategy
Quality and assurance strategy	Used to define and establish the activities for managing quality across the programme
Resource management plan	Arrangements for implementing the resource management strategy
Resource management strategy	Used to identify how the programme will acquire and manage the resources required to achieve the business change
Risk management strategy	Defines the programme approach to risk management

Title	Purpose
Risk register	Used to capture and actively manage the risks to the programme
Stakeholder engagement strategy	Used to define the framework that will enable effective stakeholder engagement and communication
Stakeholder profiles	Used to record stakeholder analysis information
Vision statement	Used to communicate the end goal of the programme; could be seen as providing an external 'artist's impression' of the desired future state

Glossary

The following terms may be used in a programme management environment. This list is a subset of the one in the MSP manual, and is a subset of the Best Practice Management PPM Portfolio Common Glossary of Terms and Definitions.

accountable

Personally answerable for an activity. Accountability cannot be delegated, unlike responsibility.

aggregated risk

The overall level of risk to the programme when all the risks are viewed as a totality rather than individually. This could include the outputs of particular scenarios or risk combinations.

as-is state

The current operating structure and performance of the parts of the business which will be impacted by a programme.

assumption

A statement that is taken as being true for the purposes of planning, but which could change later. An assumption is made where some facts are not yet known. There is a risk that assumptions are not correct.

assurance

All the systematic actions necessary to provide confidence that the target (system, process, organization, programme, project, outcome, benefit, capability, product output, deliverable) is appropriate. Appropriateness might be defined subjectively or objectively in different circumstances. The implication is that assurance will have a level of independence from that which is being assured.

baseline
A reference level against which an entity is monitored and controlled.

benefit
The measurable improvement resulting from an outcome perceived as an advantage by one or more stakeholders, and which contributes towards one or more organizational objective(s).

benefits management
The identification, definition, tracking, realization and optimization of benefits within and beyond a programme.

benefits register
Summary document that contains key information from the benefit profiles.

best practice
A defined and proven method of managing events effectively.

border
The time-bound limitations of a tranche, i.e. when end-of-tranche reviews are held and the programme receives endorsement to move into the next tranche.

boundary
The scope of what a programme will cover; the extent of its influence and authority.

business as usual (BAU)

The way the business normally achieves its objectives.

business case management

The manner in which a programme's rationale, objectives, benefits and risks are balanced against the financial investment, and how this balance is maintained, adjusted and assessed during the programme.

business change manager (BCM)

The role responsible for benefits management, from identification through to realization, and for ensuring that the implementation and embedding of the new capabilities are delivered by the projects. Typically allocated to more than one individual and also known as 'change agent'.

business change team

A group of specialists appointed to support a business change manager in the business change management aspects of benefits realization.

capability

The completed set of project outputs required to deliver an outcome; this exists prior to transition. It is a service, function or operation that enables the organization to exploit opportunities.

change manager

Reports to the business change manager (BCM) and may operate at a project level to support benefits realization, namely focus on the realization of a particular benefit.

configuration

A generic term used to describe a group of products or items that work together to deliver a product or service, or a recognizable part of a product or service. A configuration may be a configuration item of a larger configuration.

configuration item

An asset that is subject to configuration management. The asset may be a component of a product, a product, or a set of products in a release.

configuration management

Technical and administrative activities concerned with the creation, maintenance and controlled change of configuration throughout the life of a product.

consult

To give groups or individuals the opportunity to contribute to and make recommendations on an action or document.

corporate governance

The ongoing activity of maintaining a sound system of internal control by which the directors and officers of an organization ensure that effective management systems, including financial monitoring and control systems, have been put in place to protect assets, earning capacity and the reputation of the organization.

corporate portfolio

The totality of the change initiatives within an organization; it may comprise a number of programmes, standalone projects and other initiatives that achieve congruence of change.

corporate portfolio board

One name for the body within the organization that has authority to make decisions about the composition and prioritization of the organization's portfolio of programmes and projects. This may be the corporate board, and in Management of Portfolios (MoP™) it is also referred to as the 'portfolio direction group' or 'investment committee'.

cross-organizational programme

A programme requiring the committed involvement of more than one organization to achieve the desired outcomes; also referred to as a 'cross-cutting' programme.

dependency

An activity, output or decision that is required to achieve some aspect of the programme. It can be internal or external to the programme.

dis-benefit

A measurable decline resulting from an outcome perceived as negative by one or more stakeholders, which reduces one or more organizational objective(s).

emergent programme

A programme that subsumes one or more pre-existing projects into a coherent alignment with corporate policy and strategy.

end goal

The ultimate objective of a programme – the same as the 'to-be state' or 'future state'.

feedback log

A document that is used to capture, track and ensure that all stakeholder feedback is dealt with.

gated review

A structured review of a project, programme or portfolio as part of formal governance arrangements carried out at key decision points in the lifecycle to ensure that the decision to invest as per the agreed business case remains valid.

governance

The functions, responsibilities, processes and procedures that define how a programme is set up, managed and controlled.

inform

In the context of a RACI table, to advise a group or individual of a change or a decision. In MSP, this is typically used in the context of something that affects activities or document creation.

issue

A relevant event that has happened, was not planned and requires management action. It could be a problem, query, concern, change request or risk that has occurred.

key performance indicator (KPI)

A metric (either financial or non-financial) that is used to set and measure progress towards an organizational objective.

leadership

The ability to direct, influence and motivate others towards a better outcome.

margin

The flexibility that a programme has for achieving its blueprint, benefits and business case.

opportunity

An uncertain event that could have a favourable impact on objectives or benefits.

outcome

The result of change, normally affecting real-world behaviour or circumstances. Outcomes are desired when a change is conceived. Outcomes are achieved as a result of the activities undertaken to effect the change; they are the manifestation of part or all of the new state conceived in the blueprint.

output

The tangible or intangible artefact produced, constructed or created as a result of a planned activity.

P3M3

The Portfolio, Programme and Project Management Maturity Model that provides a framework with which organizations can assess their current performance and put in place improvement plans.

plan

A detailed proposal for doing or achieving something, detailing the what, when, how and by whom.

policy

A course of action (or principle) adopted by an organization; a business statement of intent, setting the tone for an organization's culture.

portfolio
The totality of an organization's investment (or segment thereof) in the changes required to achieve its strategic objectives.

product
An input or output, whether tangible or intangible, that can be described in advance, created and tested; also known as an output or deliverable.

programme
A temporary flexible organization structure created to coordinate, direct and oversee the implementation of a set of related projects and activities in order to deliver outcomes and benefits related to an organization's strategic objectives. A programme is likely to have a life that spans several years.

programme assurance
Independent assessment and confirmation that the programme as a whole or any one of its aspects is on track, that it is applying relevant practices and procedures, and that the projects, activities and business rationale remain aligned to the programme's objectives. *See also* gated review.

programme board
A group that is established to support a senior responsible owner in delivering a programme.

programme management
The coordinated organization, direction and implementation of a dossier of projects and transformation activities (i.e. the programme) to achieve outcomes and realize benefits of strategic importance.

programme manager

The role responsible for the set-up, management and delivery of a programme; typically allocated to a single individual.

programme office

The function providing the information hub and standards custodian for a programme and its delivery objectives; it could provide support for more than one programme.

programme organization

How a programme will be managed throughout its lifecycle, the roles and responsibilities of individuals involved in the programme, and personnel management or human resources arrangements. Also known as programme organization structure.

project

A temporary organization that is created for the purpose of delivering one or more business outputs according to a specified business case.

project register

An alternative term for 'projects dossier' – the document that records the list of projects.

proximity

(Of risk) the time factor and how close an event is; i.e. risks will occur at particular times, and the severity of their impact will vary depending on when they occur.

quality

The degree to which the features and inherent or assigned characteristics of a product, person, process, service and/or system bear on its ability to show that it meets expectations or stated needs, requirements or specification.

quality control

The process of monitoring specific results to determine whether they comply with the relevant standards, and of identifying ways to eliminate causes of unsatisfactory performance.

quality management system

The complete set of quality standards, procedures and responsibilities for a site or organization.

register

A formal repository that is managed and requires agreement by the board on its format, composition and use.

responsible

Used to describe the individual who has the authority and is expected to deliver a task or activity; responsibility can be delegated.

risk

An uncertain event or set of events that, should it occur, will have an effect on the achievement of objectives. A risk is measured by a combination of the probability of a perceived threat or opportunity occurring and the magnitude of its impact on objectives.

risk appetite
The amount of risk the organization, or subset of it, is willing to accept.

risk assessment
The identification and evaluation of risks.

risk estimation
The estimation of probability and impact of an individual risk, taking into account predetermined standards, target risk levels, interdependencies and other relevant factors.

risk evaluation
The process of understanding the net effect of identified threats and opportunities on an activity when aggregated together.

risk identification
The determination of what could pose a risk; a process to describe and list sources of risk (threats and opportunities).

risk management
The systematic application of principles, approaches and processes to the tasks of identifying and assessing risks, and then planning and implementing risk responses.

senior responsible owner (SRO)
The single individual with overall responsibility for ensuring that a project or programme meets its objectives and delivers the projected benefits.

sponsor
The main driving force behind a programme or project. Some organizations use the term sponsor instead of SRO.

sponsoring group

The driving force behind a programme, which provides the investment decision and top-level endorsement for the rationale and objectives of the programme.

stakeholder

Any individual, group or organization that can affect, be affected by, or perceives itself to be affected by, a programme.

stakeholder map

A diagrammatic representation of the stakeholders relevant to an organizational activity and their respective interests.

stakeholder register

A document that contains a summary of the information in the stakeholder profiles.

strategy

An approach or line to take, designed to achieve a long-term aim. Strategies can exist at different levels in an organization – in MSP there are corporate strategies for achieving objectives that will give rise to programmes. Programmes then develop strategies aligned with these corporate objectives against particular delivery areas.

threat

An uncertain event that could have a negative impact on objectives or benefits.

to-be state

The future planned state of an organization as described by the blueprint.

tranche

A programme management term describing a group of projects structured around distinct step changes in capability and benefit delivery.

transformation

A distinct change to the way an organization conducts all or part of its business.

transition plan

The schedule of activities to cover the 'transition' phase of the benefits realization plan.

vision

A picture of a better future that will be delivered by the programme.

workstream

The logical grouping of projects and activities that together enable effective management. Workstreams may delineate projects against a variety of criteria.